The Longman Book Projec

Language 2

Language Book 1

Sue Palmer

with a Glossary of words about language
by
David Crystal
Consultant: Wendy Body

This is part of
THE LONGMAN BOOK PROJECT
General Editor Sue Palmer
Fiction Editor Wendy Body
Non-fiction Editor Bobbie Neate

LONGMAN GROUP LIMITED
Longman House, Burnt Mill, Harlow, Essex, CM20 2JE, England
and Associated Companies throughout the World.
Text © Sue Palmer

Second impression 1995
ISBN 0 582 12454 9
Printed and bound in Great Britain by Lawrence Allen (Colour Printers) Western-Super-Mare, Avon

The publisher's policy is to use paper manufactured from sustainable forests.

CONTENTS

Looking at language

Glossary Check
extract
language

There are 11 units in this book.
Each unit starts with an **extract** from a *Longman Book Project* book. The extracts are for you to read and enjoy. We hope they will tempt you to find the books they come from and to read or reread them for yourself.

The extracts have also been chosen for another reason. They are all good examples of written **language.** We can look at them to find out more about how language works and the different ways it can be used.

Why bother looking at language?

Language is a very, very important part of our lives.
Think for a moment what life would be like if we could not

speak   listen

read   write.

We use language almost all the time. The trouble is, we are usually so busy *using* language that we don't stop to think about it.
This book gives you a chance to stop and think about language. In each unit we put part of language "under the magnifying glass" and learn more about it.

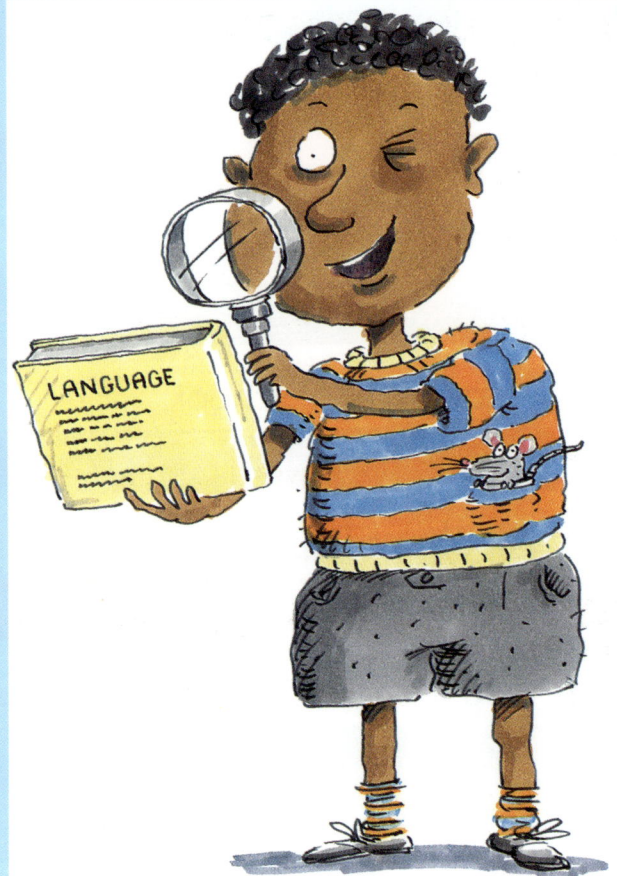

LANGUAGE

Words about language

When you are learning about language, you need words to talk about it. The words you need to know for each unit are in a Glossary Check box at the top of the page. When we use these words for the first time in the unit, we put them in **bold print**. You will find the meanings of these words in the **glossary** at the back of the book.

As you learn more and more words about language, you can build up your own personal glossary.

Booklet **C** 21–24
Word meanings **C** 25–26
(Further details in Teacher's Resource Book, pp.16–18)

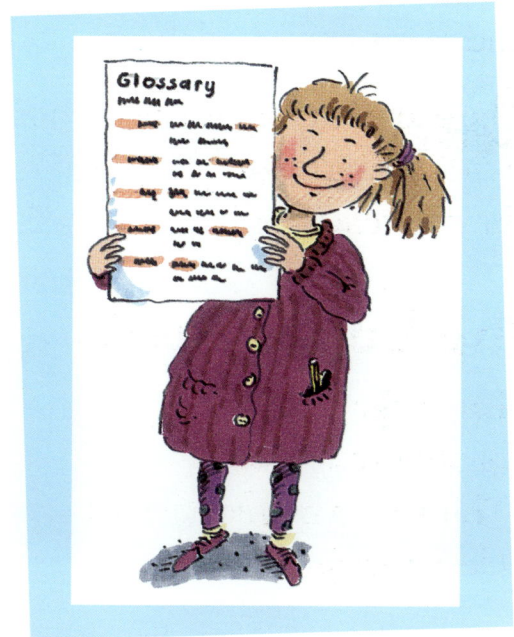

Using this book

The **Talkabout** sections are for you to learn about language with your teacher.

The **Practice** sections have activities to help you remember new words and ideas.

The **Into Action** sections have more activities for writing or experimenting with language. These activities give you a chance to put what you have learned into action.

There will be lots of other opportunities to put what you know about language into action – every day when you are

reading   writing   speaking   listening.

How babies grow

A six-month-old baby

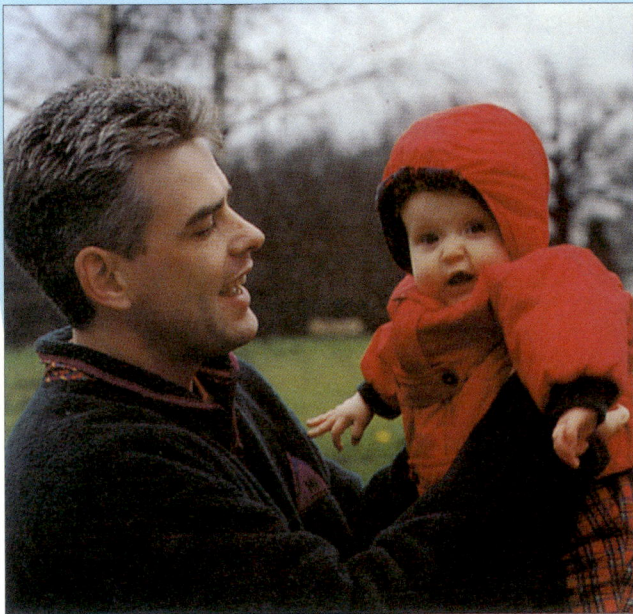

Paul can sit up and he loves to play with toys. He likes to put things in his mouth to taste them, and to feel whether they are hard or soft.

Paul cannot talk but he makes lots of noises that sound like real words. He understands some words that his family uses. When he is about 9 months old he will say his first word.

A one-year-old baby

Mai Ling can walk ten steps. She can now pick up small things with her thumb and finger. She can also pull toys along with a string. She can even scribble with a pencil. She can say ten real words and she understands lots of words.

A two-year-old toddler

Most two-year-olds can talk, walk and run.

How a baby develops

	Newborn	6 weeks	3 months	6 months	one year	two years
Physical Development		smiles	rolls over	crawls a little sits up	crawling walking a little	walks steadily runs
Play		looks at bright objects	can hold rattles	likes to drop toys	plays with simple toys	plays with many toys
Language Development	cries	gurgles cries	coos – coo-coo laughs	babbles bababa dadada	first word mama	says two words together dada gone
Food	only milk	only milk	a very little baby food lots of milk	finger foods, soft foods milk	mashed up meat, fish, eggs, cheese	family meals cut up into pieces

From *How babies grow* by Bobbie Neate and Susan Henry (LBP Non-Fiction 1 – Babies)

Talkabout

Sense and sentences

Most of the extract about "How babies grow" is written in **sentences**.
Each one starts with a **capital letter** and ends with a **full stop**.

- How many sentences are there in each of the three sections?
- Which is the longest sentence? Which is the shortest?
- Why do you think people write in sentences?

The writing in the **chart** is not in complete sentences.

- How can you tell?
- Try putting the information in the chart into sentences.
- Why do you think the chart is not written in sentences?

Baby talk

When babies first learn to speak, they do not make grown-up sentences. They just put two or three words together. Sometimes it is hard to understand what they mean.

Here are some bits of baby talk:

Daddy sock   **Mummy drink**
no walk   **cat byebyes**
doggy out   **all gone dinner**

Mummy dinner!

- What might the bits of baby talk mean?
- Can you think of more than one meaning for each?
- Try making them into grown-up sentences.

Practice

Sentences make sense

1 Copy out these sentences. Give each of them a capital letter at the beginning and a full stop at the end.

a sentence makes sense

a written sentence starts with a capital letter

most sentences end with a full stop

2 Make a chart like this in your book.

Sentences	Not sentences

Put these groups of words under the correct heading in your chart:

Mai Ling can walk ten steps

can hold rattles

a very little baby food

Paul sits up.

Most two year olds can walk and talk.

A two-year-old toddler

New born

Newborn babies cry.

plays with many toys.

3 Work out what you think these bits of baby talk mean. Make them into grown-up sentences, and write them in your book. Remember capital letters and full stops.

a) no play ball

b) mummy bed

c) bad cat scratch

d) baby home

More practice/revision: C 1
Link to *Spelling and Handwriting Workbook One*, pages 3–6

Into Action

The sentence game

Any number of people – two or more – can play this game.

- Sit in a row.
- The first person says a word to start off a sentence.
- The next person has to supply the next word, and so on.
- When you reach the end of a sentence, the next player says "Full stop, capital letter."
- Then the next player starts off another sentence.

I   like   dogs   full stop capital letter   red   flowers   are   very

Spelling-sentences

Spelling-sentences can help you remember tricky spelling words.

p e o p l e

People eat orange peel like elephants.

Use the letters of the word **c o u l d** to make up a silly sentence. Draw a picture to help you remember it.

Now try it with one of these words:

because   answer   know

How language grows

> When I was one, I was just begun.
> When I was two, I was nearly new.
> When I was three, I was hardly me.
> When I was four, I was not much more.
> When I was five, I was just alive.
> But now I am six, I'm as clever as clever,
> So I think I'll be six now for ever and ever!
>
> A.A. Milne

Find out about the language development of babies or young children you know.

**Can they talk yet?   Can they link words together?
Can they make sentences?**

If not, can you help them make what they say into sentences?

Baby talk

A game for 2 to 4 players

You need:
21 small cards in three piles of 7

Copy the words on the right on to one side of the cards. Number the cards 1, 2 or 3 on the other sides.

Pile 1	Pile 2	Pile 3
Mummy	jump	ball
Daddy	wash	dish
me	play	dinner
dog	eat	apple
cat	drink	bed
baby	take	book
Grandma	go	kitchen

How to play

- Put the three piles of cards on the table, word-side down.
- Each player takes one card from each pile to make a "baby-talk" sentence.
- The player must then make this into a sensible grown-up sentence.
- If the player can make a grown-up sentence, s/he keeps the cards.
- If there are any words which the player cannot fit into the sentence, s/he should put them back at the bottom of the pile they came from.
- Play the game until all the cards have gone. The player with the most cards at the end is the winner.

All the king's things

There once was a grumpy King. His name was King Grumpyguts, and he never smiled or laughed.

I don't know why he's so grumpy. He's got an enormous palace and the finest gardens that money can buy.

All this belongs to the King!

He's got lakes, rivers, trees. Everything he could possibly want.

He's even got his very own wildlife park...

Even more things.

Gold plated motorbike

Diamonds on his rollerskates.

In fact King grumpyguts had everything. Well everything but one. He didn't have happiness. He was not a happy king.

From *King Grumpyguts* by Stan Cullimore, illustrated by Peter Kavanagh. (LBP Fiction 2, Band 1)

Talkabout

Nouns

We need **nouns** to talk about the people, places, things, animals and ideas in the King Grumpyguts picture-story. Here are some

| king | jester | dog | map | palace | bus | happiness |

How many more **nouns** can you find in the picture-story?

Practice

Nouns are names

1 Write down 10 nouns from the picture-story.

2 Draw a picture of some of the nouns in your life.
Show people, places, objects and animals that are important to you.
Label them with nouns, like in our picture:

telephone
crown
nose
dog
squirrel
bone
signpost
King
grass
leaf
bike

3 Copy out this bit from the story. Underline all the nouns. We have started you off. There are 5 more.

King Grumpyguts has got an enormous palace and the finest gardens that money can buy. He's got lakes, rivers, trees.

Dream nouns

Imagine you were a king or queen and you could do anything in the world.
Make four lists of nouns.

people I would meet	places I would go	things I would own	animals I would keep

Compare your list with a friend's list. Talk about why you have each chosen the nouns on your lists.

ABC of nouns

Make a tiny book called **"ABC of nouns"**, with a page for each letter of the alphabet. Draw a picture of a person, place, thing or animal for each letter and label it.

How to make a tiny abc book

1. Get two sheets of A4 paper.

2. Fold both sheets into 4 quarters.

3. Cut along the folds so you have 8 small pieces of paper.

4. You only need 7 of these pieces to make your book. Put them into a neat pile.

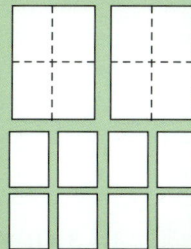

5. Fold the sheets into a book shape.

Happy thought

Copy this poem in your best handwriting. All round it, draw some of the things that make you happy.

The world is so full
of a number of things
I'm sure we should all
be as happy as kings.
Robert Louis Stevenson

Billy Blue

Billy Blue lived on an island , all alone with a coconut tree that he talked to, called Sam.
One day it was Billy Blue's birthday. "I'll have a _____," said Billy,
but he couldn't have much of a party all by himself, with a tree, so…
the elephants came in an elephant boat
and the crocodiles came in a crocodile plane
and the hippos came in a hippocopter
and the monkeys came on the back of a whale
and the little birds came on the wind .

You can find the complete story in *"Billy Blue's Birthday"* in *Billy Fishbone and other sea stories*
by Martin Waddell, illustrated by Reg Cartwright (LBP Fiction 2, Band 1)

Nouns and proper nouns

Someone has covered up lots of the nouns in the bit of story on page 16.
What do you think the missing nouns are?

a boy called Billy Blue

a tree called Sam

Billy Blue is a **proper noun**. It is the special name of a particular boy.

Sam is a **proper noun**. It is the special name of a particular tree!

All **proper nouns** should be written with a capital letter at the beginning. Here are some more:

King Grumpyguts   **Scotland**   **Bambi**
Martin Waddell   **North Sea**

Your name is a proper noun. So are the names of your friends, your pets, your school and the place you live.
Write some proper nouns from your life on the board.

Our teacher is called Mrs Moon.
I am Tanya.
My name is Patrick.

My name is Ishmael.
I have a dog called Patch.
We live in Belfast.

Make up good names for the elephants, crocodiles and other animals in the picture on page 16.
Write these proper nouns on the board too.

Practice Oo **Proper nouns and capital letters**

1 Copy these sentences, filling in the missing proper nouns.

My name is
My teacher is called
The place where I live is called
The name of my favourite animal is
If I had a tree, I would call it
My four best friends are called

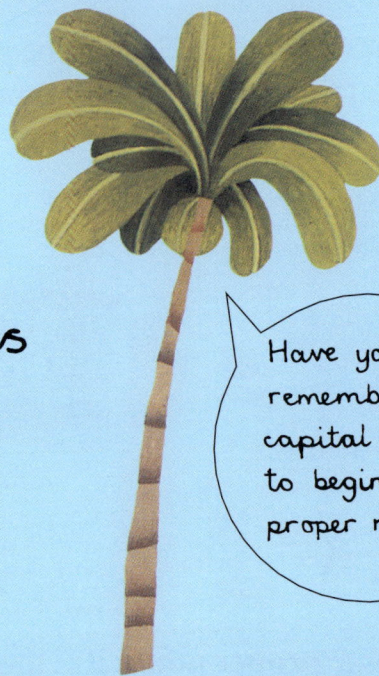

Have you remembered capital letters to begin proper nouns?

The elephants are
called Mumbo and Jumbo.
The crocodiles are
called Snip and Snap.
The hippos are called
Alice and Angus.
The monkeys are

2 The picture shows how a girl called Emma named some of the animals in the Billy Blue story. Choose good names for all the animals and write them in your book in the way Emma wrote hers.

3 Here is an extract from another story by Martin Waddell.
We have missed out 6 capital letters for proper nouns.
Copy the passage, putting in the capital letters.

billy fishbone and his sister bianca sailed on a
broken-down boat called minerva somewhere
out on the barnacle sea.

Guess the noun

Write a story of your own about:

> My island or
>
> A birthday party

- Choose some of the nouns in your story and cover them up with sticky tape or pieces of Blu-tack.

- Can your friends guess what the nouns are?

Proper noun families

Alice Adams   **Alfred Adams**

The Adams family from Aberdeen

Andrew   **Amy**

The Barton family from Barbados

Brinsley   **Bella**

Ben Barton **Beatrice Barton**

Think of families for other letters of the alphabet, and write them down.
How many families can you make?
Don't forget the capital letters!

My name is …

My name is **Sluggery-Wuggery**
My name is **Worms-For-Tea**
My name is **Swallow-The-Table-Leg**
My name is **Drink-The-Sea.**

My name is **I-Eat-Saucepans**
My name is **I-Like-Snails**
My name is **Grand-Piano-George**
My name is **I-Ride-Whales**

My name is **Jump-The-Chimney**
My name is **Bite-My-Kee**
My name is **Jiggery-Pokery**
And **Riddle-Me-Ree, and ME.**

Pauline Clarke

Who or what do you think the owner(s) of these names might be? Draw pictures of your favourites.

With a partner, make up a poem like this one, with lots of funny names in it. (Your poem does not have to rhyme.) Draw pictures to go with your poem.

Don't forget capital letters for proper nouns!

Has it gone off?

Here are some pictures of food.
Which of these foods are good to eat?
Which of these foods are bad?

↥This bread has just been sliced.

Do you think that this bread looks stale?

↥It's best to feel the fruit gently before you eat it.

Do you think that these peaches feel soft?

↥ These fish are lying on a bed of ice to keep them cool.

Do you think that these fish smell fresh?

↥It is difficult to tell if this milk is fresh or not.

Do you think that this milk tastes sour?

From *Has it gone off?* by Ann Langran and Mark Nutting, (LBP Non-Fiction 1–Food)

Talkabout

Questions and statements

How many **sentences** can you find on the opposite page?
How many are **questions**?
How many are **statements**?
How do you know the difference between questions and statements in writing?

- Let a few people read the page aloud.
  Listen for differences in the way people use their voices:

    – when they are asking questions
    – when they are making statements.

How can you tell from someone's voice that they are asking a question?

Read the sentences in the box aloud and decide which are questions and which are statements.
What is missing from each sentence?

stale bread makes good toast   **do you like fruit**

why are the fish lying on ice   **is the bread stale**

fresh peaches smell lovely   **milk is white**

Look back to pages 6–7.
Make up some questions about the information there.
The "question words" in the box might help you.

what where why when

where how who which

Make up statements to answer your questions.
Make sure all your statements are complete sentences.

Practice

1   Copy these sentences, giving each one
     a capital letter for the first word
     a full stop or a question mark.

do you like bread
there are five peaches on the plate
here is a glass of milk
what do you want to eat
how fresh are those fish

2   Write down 5 questions about the extracts you have read in this book so far. Don't forget the question marks.

3   Here are some statements which are answers to questions. Work out what the questions are and write them down. We have done the first one to show you how.

a) **Grass is green.**   What colour is grass?
b) **Dogs eat meat.**
c) **The king lives in a palace.**
d) **My name is Billy Blue.**
e) **I am eight years old.**

Into Action

Getting to know you

Draw a line down the middle of a sheet of paper. On the left-hand side, write 10 questions that will help you get to know someone better. Then find someone you don't know very well (perhaps a child from a younger class). Ask them your questions and write down their answers.

More practice/revision: **C** 4
Link to *Spelling and Handwriting Workbook One*, pages 15–18

Ask a silly question... get a silly answer

- Play this game with a partner.
- One of you is "It". The other is the questioner.
- The questioner asks "It" questions – they can be as silly as you like.
- "It" has to answer them, but the answers must be wrong.
- When "It" gets an answer right, s/he has lost the game.
- Swap over so that the other partner is "It".

What colour is the sun?

The sun is purple with blue spots.

Quiz questions

Choose a **non-fiction** book from the book corner. Look through it carefully.

- Then write down 5 questions which you know the book will answer.
- Give the book and your questions to a friend.
- Can s/he answer all your questions?

What is ...?

What is pink? A rose is pink
  by the fountain's brink.
What is red? A poppy's red
  in its barley bed.
What is blue? The sky is blue
  where the clouds float thro'.
What is white? A swan is white
  sailing in the light.
What is yellow? Pears are yellow,
  rich and ripe and mellow.
What is green? The grass is green,
  with small flowers between.
What is violet? Clouds are violet
  in the summer twilight.
What is orange? Why, an orange,
  just an orange!

Christina Rossetti

Practise reading this poem with a partner, one of you reading the questions and the other reading the statements.
Then swap over.
With your partner, make up a poem of your own like this one.
Make up some questions (as strange as you like!) and some answers (as strange as you like!) and set them out like a poem.
Your poem doesn't have to rhyme.

Cockadoodle – what?!

a play by Geraldine McCaughrean

Characters:

A narrator

Cockerel Peck – the farmyard cock

Gregorie Peck – his wife

Good Dog – a sheepdog

Blue Moo – a cow

Tally-Ho – a horse

Baabra Lamb – a young sheep

Farmer Harry

Everything happens in the farmyard of Home Farm. Cockerel Peck's bed stays in the middle of the stage from start to end. He is in it.

SCENE 1

Narrator	It is morning at Home Farm. The sun is just coming up. The animals are all asleep. Someone must wake them up. Cockerel Peck will do it, of course... Won't he?

(An alarm clock rings. Gregorie Peck sits up and gives Cockerel Peck a push so that he falls out of bed.)

Cockerel	Huh? What's happening? What's the matter?
Gregorie	It's morning. Time to crow. You mustn't be late.
Cockerel	Morning? *Again*? It always seems to be morning.
Narrator	And Cockerel Peck got back into bed.
Gregorie	What are you doing?
Cockerel	I'm going back to sleep. I'm tired out. I'm sick of getting up so early. Why should I?
Gregorie	But you must! The animals won't wake up! Farmer Harry won't wake up! The milk will be late! The eggs!
Cockerel	Don't care.

(He pulls the covers over his head.)

Gregorie   Well! I don't know! You lazy, idle, good-for-nothing bird! I suppose I must do your work for you. As I always say, if a thing needs doing, do it yourself. So I will ⋯ Cock-a-doodle-puck-puck-puck!

(Enter Good Dog)

Good Dog   That's not right.

Gregorie   Good morning, Good Dog. My lazy husband doesn't want to get up. So I am crowing for him this morning. Cock-a-doodle-puck-puck-puck!

(Blue Moo comes in)

Blue Moo   That's not right.

Gregorie   Good morning, Blue Moo. My lazy, good-for-nothing husband doesn't want to get up . So I am crowing for him this morning. Cock-a-doodle-puck-puck-puck!

(Tally-Ho comes in)

Tally-Ho   That's not right.

Gregorie   Good morning, Tally-Ho Horse. My lazy, idle, good-for-nothing husband doesn't want to get up. So I am crowing for him this morning. Cock-a-doodle-puck-puck-puck!

(Baabra Lamb comes in)

Baabra   That's not right.

Gregorie   Good morning, Baabra Lamb. My lazy, idle, good-for-nothing, worthless husband doesn't want to get up. So I am crowing today. Cock-a-doodle-puck-puck-puck!

Baabra   What fun! Can I try?

Gregorie   Fun? Fun! I'm not doing this for fun. I am doing it because my husband is too... too... too...

Cockerel   *Tired !*

(He puts his head back under the covers)

Baabra   Well, I don't mind taking my turn.

Good Dog   What a good idea. We can all take turns.

Gregorie   You?

Blue Moo   Cock-a-doodle-moooooo!

Cockerel   It sounds like a very good idea to me. Here is the alarm clock.
Now will everybody please leave me alone and let me sleep?

SCENE TWO

Narrator   So every morning a different animal in the farmyard takes a turn to wake the others.

(Blue Moo comes in)

Blue Moo   Cock-a-doodle-moooooo! (and goes out)

(Good Dog comes in)

Good Dog   Cock-a-doodle-woof-woof! (and goes out)

(Baabra Lamb comes in)

Baabra   Cock-a-doodle-baaaaa! (and goes out)

(Tally-Ho comes in)

Tally-Ho   Cock-a-doodle-neigh-hay-hay! (and goes out)

(Gregorie comes in)

Gregorie   Oh the shame of it! The shame! All these animals taking the place of Cockerel Peck.
If my mother only knew!
Owowowo!

SCENE THREE

Narrator   But the animals are not used to getting up so early. Cockerel Peck's alarm clock rings each morning. But they still find it very hard to wake up. And the farmyard is *very* dark.

(Blue Moo comes in)

Blue Moo   Cock-a-doodle-mooo!

(She goes out crowing. There is a loud squelch. Good Dog comes in)

Good Dog   What was that? Oh dear! Blue Moo has fallen in the sheep dip. I had better do her crowing this morning. Cock-a-doodle-woof-woof!

(He goes out crowing. There is a loud splash. Baabra Lamb comes in)

Baabra   What was that? Oh dear! Good Dog has walked into the milk churns. I had better do his crowing this morning. Cock-a-doodle-baaaa!

(She goes out crowing. There is a loud splash. Tally-Ho comes in)

Tally-Ho   What was that? Oh dear! Baabra Lamb has fallen in the duck pond. I had better do her crowing this morning. Tally-ho! Cock-a-doodle-neigh-hay-hay!

(He goes out crowing. There is a loud clatter)

Narrator   All the noise brought Farmer Harry to the bedroom window.

Farmer   What was that? Good heavens! Come and see, Doris. Tally-Ho the horse is in our dog's kennel! How? I don't know how. He just is. Come and see. The horse is in the kennel! What time is it? Dear me, it's time for milking. I wonder why I keep on waking up late recently.

27

Narrator	And Farmer Harry went off to get ready for work. He didn't see the other animals coming back. Blue Moo had a bucket on her head. Good-Dog was all milky. Baabra Lamb was covered in pond weed. Tally-Ho had a bone in his mouth. They were all groaning.

(All the animals come in)

Good Dog	Oh dear. This is awful.
Tally-Ho	Oh dear. This is dreadful.
Blue Moo	Oh dear. This is terrible.
Baabra	Oh dear. What am I going to do?
Cockerel	Please! How can I sleep with all this noise? What is the matter, Good Dog?
Good Dog	Moo-oo.
Cockerel	Moo? Good Dog, did you just moo like a cow? You did! Did you hear him, Blue Moo?
Blue Moo	Baaaa.
Cockerel	Blue Moo? You bleated like a sheep. You did! Did you hear him, Baabra Lamb?
Baabra	Quack.
Cockerel	Quack?
Tally-Ho	Woof woof.
Cockerel	Not you too, Tally-Ho? Good Dog moos like a cow. Blue Moo bleats like a sheep. Tally-Ho barks like a dog. And Baabra Lamb quacks like a duck. What happened?
Good Dog	I walked into the milk churns. Mooo!
Blue Moo	I fell into the sheep dip. Baa!
Tally-Ho	I ran into Good Dog's kennel. Woof!

Baabra	I fell in the duck pond. Quack!
Cockerel	I'm confused.
Gregorie	This is all your fault.
Cockerel	*My* fault?
Gregorie	Of course. If you weren't so lazy, none of this would have happened.
Cockerel	I'm sorry. I just needed a holiday. Everyone needs a holiday. I'll go back to work tomorrow.
Good Dog	This is awful. Farmer Harry will try to milk me. Give me back my bark, Tally-Ho!
Blue Moo	This is terrible. Farmer Harry will try to shear me for wool. Give me back my moo, Good-Dog!
Tally-Ho	This is dreadful. Farmer Harry will want me to herd the sheep. Where is my neigh?
Baabra	Oh dear. I can't swim like a duck. I'll probably drown. Give me back my bleat, Blue Moo!
Gregorie	Hush. Listen. All your noises are mixed up. It's simple. We must simply sort them out again. Let's all join hands and make a circle... Now dance... *Faster... FASTER!*

(Farmer Harry comes in)

Farmer	Good morning, animals. I am glad to see you so happy. But it is rather late. Blue Moo, come with me to the milking shed!
Blue Moo	Mooo.
Narrator	It worked!
Farmer	Tally-Ho, here's a sack of oats for you.
Tally-Ho	Neigh-hay-hay.
Narrator	Thank goodness!
Farmer	Baabra Lamb, what are you doing here in the farmyard?
Baabra	Baaa-ha-ha-ha-ha-ha!
Farmer	Good Dog, be a good dog and take her back to the field.
Good Dog	Woof woof.
Narrator	Phew!
Farmer	And you, Gregorie Peck? When are you going to lay me a nice egg for my breakfast?

Quack.

Gregorie	Quack.
All	Quack?
Gregorie	Quack-quack-quack-quack-quack!
	(The End)

You can read more about the animals in the farmyard in *Gregorie Peck, Blue Moo, Good Dog* and *Baabra Lamb* by Geraldine McCaughrean illustrated by Colin Smithson (LBP Fiction 2, Bands 1 and 2)

Punctuation and expression

When you are reading, it is important to get the right **expression** into your voice. Looking at the **punctuation** helps you decide what sort of expression you need.

Different sorts of sentences need different sorts of expression.

It's morning.
Time to crow.

Why should I?

Statement
Punctuation mark = full stop ●

Question
Punctuation mark = question mark **?**

Well I don't know!
You lazy, idle, good-for-nothing bird!

Exclamation
Punctuation mark = exclamation mark **!**

Find some **statements**, **questions** and **exclamations** in the play *Cockadoodle-what!?* Read them with the right sort of expression in your voice.

Sometimes a sentence is interrupted...

I'm crowing because my husband is too...too...too...

Tired!

Sometimes sentences trail off...

Let's all join hands and make a circle

Now dance...

Faster...FASTER

Glossary Check

dots
emphasis
underlining
italic print

Find more **unfinished sentences** in the play.
Why do you think that each of these sentences is unfinished?

Which words in the speeches above should be **emphasized?**

Find more examples of **emphasis** in the play.
Why do you think the speaker wants to emphasize the words each time?

Practise reading the play in groups.
Use the punctuation to help you get the right sort of expression into your voices.

When you have practised, perhaps you could make a tape or video-recording of your performance.
Then listen to decide if you are reading with expression.

Practice Punctuation helps you read well.

1 Copy out this extract from the play. Put in punctuation marks where they have been missed out (. ? ! ...) Underline any words which you think should be emphasised.

Baabra	What fun Can I try
Gregorie	Fun Fun
	I'm not doing this for fun
	I'm doing it because my husband is too too too
Cockerel	Tired
Baabra	Well, I don't mind taking my turn
Good Dog	What a good idea
	We can all take turns
Gregorie	You

Check back to the play to see if your punctuation is the same as the author's.

2

> One day, Baabra Lamb lost her tail, and asked Cockerel Peck if he had seen it. Cockerel was trying to get some sleep, so he was cross with Baabra. Then Gregorie came and told him off.

Write a little play to tell the story in the box above.

Set it out like the *Cockadoodle – what?!* play.

Put in punctuation marks to show how it should be read.

Can you use all the different punctuation marks we have learned about?

You could start like this...

Baabra	Please, Cockerel Peck, have you seen my tail?
Cockerel	

Shadow Dance

There's a small town in France
where the shadows dance
by the dark light of the moon…

Dark shapes are
slipping
and gliding and sliding
along.
The Shadows have come to the Square and…

Dum-a-dum-dum
Dum-a-dum-dum,
the beat of a drum,
the shrill of a pipe
and the sound of a fiddle
scraping a jig
and…

Spinning
and gliding
and prancing
and springing
and leaping
by the light of the moon,
the shadows dance!

From *Shadow Dance* by Martin Waddell, illustrated by John Montgomery (LBP Fiction 2, Band 2)

Verbs

There are many verbs in *Shadow Dance* which tell us what is happening and
what the shadows **do**. Here are some of them:

slipping   gliding   come   leaping

- How many more verbs can you find on pages 34–35?
- Most verbs are about **doing** things.
- Try acting out every verb on pages 34–35.

Guess the verb

- Think of a verb, but don't tell anyone what it is.
- Act out your verb for everyone to guess.

Practice oo **What's happening?   Verbs!**

1 Think of 10 things that you can do. Write down the 10 verbs like this.

I can smile.
I can

2 Look back at the play *Cockadoodle-What*?! on pages 24–30.

Copy this list of the characters from the play:

Gregorie Peck
Good - Dog
Blue Moo
Tally - Ho
Baabra Lamb
Farmer Harry

Write two verbs beside each name, to show two things that the character does in the play.
The first one is done for you, to show you how.

3 Copy this passage. Underline all the verbs. We have started you off.
There are 5 more.

They are spinning and gliding and prancing
and springing and leaping by the light of the
moon. The shadows dance.

Animal verbs

Choose an animal.

Make a list of as many verbs as possible that go with that animal.

Think of
- how your animal eats and sleeps
- the different ways it moves around
- the sorts of noises it makes
- how it uses different parts of its face and body
- anything else special about your animal.

Who can make the longest list of verbs? Use your verbs to write a poem about your animal.

Made-up verbs

Make up some verbs of your own, and decide what they mean.

Mime them for your friends.

I like to **groggle**

Do you like **blittering**

I'm going to **splodge** you

Sing a song of verbs

You can put different verbs into snatches of songs – like this one.
Sing it round the class as a game.

Oh, I just **picked up** a baby bumble bee…
Won't my mummy be so very proud of me!

Oh, I just **drew** a baby bumble bee…
Won't my mummy be so very proud of me!

Oh, I just **swatted** a baby bumble bee…
Won't my mummy be so very proud of me!

Oh, I just **tickled** a baby bumble bee…
Won't my mummy be so very proud of me!

When the teacher gets fed up, you can all sing the last verse

OOOOOOOW!
It **stung** me.

Making shadows

You can make shadows act like puppets.

You can make shadows with your hands.
You can make them look like animals.
Shadow puppets work in the same way.

It is the patterns and holes on the puppet that make the shape of the shadow so interesting.

Making a dragon shadow puppet

You will need:

a wooden rod or cane,
about 35 cm long

8 paper fasteners (butterfly clips)

2 lengths of strong wire, both
about 30cm long

scissors

paints

a roll of sticky tape

cardboard about 40 cm long
and 30 cm wide

1 Copy the dragon shapes onto the cardboard.

2 Cut out the shapes.

3 Get a grown-up to make holes where the dots are.

4 Join the puppet together using the paper fasteners.
Match up the numbers to get the right pieces together.

5 Paint your dragon.

6 Stick the rod to the back of the dragon's chin (with the sticky tape).

7 Put a piece of wire through the dragon's chin.
Bend the wire so it cannot come out.

8 Put a piece of wire through the dragon's tail. Bend the wire.

9 Put the puppet about 60cm in front of a light shining on a wall
and you will then see its shadow.

From *Making puppets* by James Dunbar (LBP Non-Fiction 1–Toys)

Talkabout

Instructions – nouns and verbs

The **instructions** for making a shadow puppet are in two parts

things you need	**what to do**
There are lots of **nouns** here, like these	There are lots of **verbs** here, like these
rod cane wire	**copy cut get make**
Find some more. Why are there lots of nouns in the list of things you need?	Find some more. Why are there lots of verbs in the part that tells you what to do?

Find another book that gives instructions (for instance a recipe book or a book of how to make things).
Find **nouns** in the lists of things you need, and **verbs** in the parts that tell you what to do.

What sorts of things do you think are important when you are writing instructions?
What do you think makes:

good instructions	bad instructions

Think of something you can make.
Work out instructions for how to make it.
Make a list of things you need and
instructions for what to do.

oo Nouns and verbs in instructions

1 Find 10 nouns in the instructions for making a shadow puppet (on page 39).
   Make a list, starting like this:

   Ten nouns in the instructions are

2 Find 10 verbs in the instructions for making a shadow puppet.
   Make a list, starting like this:

   Ten verbs in the instructions are

3 Write instructions telling people how to make something.

Make a list of   *Things you need*

and a list of   *What you do*

You could write about how to make a folded butterfly picture (see the picture on the opposite page) or about something else you know how to make.

More practice/revision: **C** 11
Link to *Spelling and Handwriting Workbook Two*, pages 7–10

Into Action

Shadow dance puppet play

Make shadow puppets of the characters in *Shadow Dance* by Martin Waddell. Turn the story into a shadow puppet play.

Someone can read the play out, while other people work the puppets.

My shadow

I have a little shadow who goes
in and out with me,
And what can be the use of him
is more than I can see.
He is very, very like me from the
heels up to the head;
And I see him jump before me,
when I jump into my bed.

The funniest thing about
him is the way
he likes to grow –
Not at all like proper
children, which is
always very slow;

For he sometimes
shoots up
taller like
an india-rubber ball,
And he sometimes gets so little
there's none of him at all.

One morning, very early, before
the sun was up,
I rose and found the shining dew
on every buttercup;
But my lazy little shadow, like an
arrant sleepyhead,
Had stayed at home behind me
and was fast asleep in bed.

Robert Louis Stevenson

Practise reading
this poem with
expression.

Shadow pictures

Try making these shadow pictures:

Rabbit

Duck

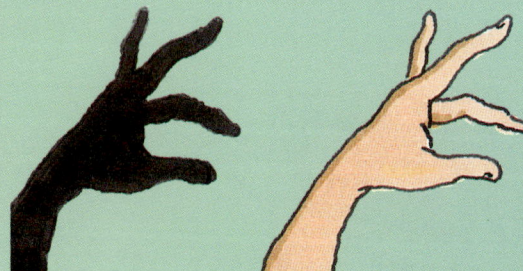

Dog

Can you invent any more shadow pictures?
Write a little booklet of instructions
for making the shadow pictures.
You could copy our diagrams
and write the instructions underneath.
Draw your own diagrams for
the shadow pictures you have made up.

Letang's new school

It was Letang's first day at school in England.

Mum and Dad waved as the headteacher took Letang across the hall.

"This is where we have our assembly," said the headteacher.

She smiled at Letang.

"You are our first child from Botswana. I'm sure you will be very happy in Ms Miller's class."

Letang did not say anything. She was thinking about assembly in her old school with her headteacher, Mrs Moyo.

A roomful of faces looked up as Ms Miller said "Hello."

"Children, this is Letang," said the headteacher.

"She has come a long way to join us. I hope you will make her feel at home."

Faces smiled and nodded. But from the corner of her eye Letang
saw two girls wrinkle their noses and grin at each other. They reminded
her of two naughty children in her old school.

From *Letang's new friend* by Beverley Naidoo, illustrated by Petra Röhr-Rouendaal (LBP Fiction 2, Band 2)

Talkabout

First and second languages

Letang's new school is in Britain. The teachers and children all speak
English. This is most people's **first language** in Britain.

At Letang's school in Botswana, the teachers and children speak Setswana.
You can see some **words** written in Setswana on the board in the picture.

Katse e rata go tsoma bommamathwane le dinoga.
(A cat   likes to hunt   bats   and snakes.)

Setswana is most people's first language in Botswana.
In Botswana, English is usually a **second language.**

Glossary Check

first language
word
second language
bilingual

Letang and her parents can speak Setswana and English.
They are **bilingual.**
Are you bilingual? Which languages can you speak?
If you are not, do you know anyone who can speak more than one language?

Another name for your **first language** is your **mother tongue.**
Why do you think it is sometimes called this?

Here are the numbers one to ten in English and Setswana. The numerals are used in both countries.

numeral	English word	Setswana word		
1	one	bongwe	(**say** bŏng-nwe)	The marks show "short vowels"
2	two	bobedi	(**say** boh-bĕ-dĭ)	
3	three	boraro	(**say** boh-rră-roh)	ă as in cat
4	four	bone	(**say** boh-nĕ)	ĕ as in bed
5	five	bothano	(**say** boh-tă-nŏ)	
6	six	borataro	(**say** boh-rră-tă-roh)	ĭ as in pin
7	seven	bosupa	(**say** boh-soo-pă)	ŏ as in pot
8	eight	boferabobedi	(**say** boh-fĕ-rră-boh-bĕ-dĭ)	ŭ as in tub
9	nine	boferabongwe	(**say** boh-fĕ-rră-boh-nwĕ)	
10	ten	lesome	(**say** lay-soh-mĕ)	

Do you know the numbers in any other languages?
Can you learn to count in a new language?

Into Action

+ and -

Try these sums in Setswana

bongwe + borataro =   boferabobedi - bothano =

Make up some sums of your own in Setswana.

(The answers must be no greater than 10.)

Swap sums with a partner and write down the answers.

Into Action

A greetings collection

Hello

Dumela mma

In English it's "Hello", in French it's "Bonjour", in Setswana it's "Dumela mma" to a girl and "Dumela rra" to a boy.
What other languages can you find out about?
Collect as many greetings as you can, from as many different languages as you can.

Invent a language

Work with a partner to make up a simple language of your own.
Start by inventing words for the numbers one to ten.
Write them down in a list.

Then make up ways of saying the words in the box below, and any other words you'd like to be able to say:

hello	how many	fingers	boys
goodbye	where are	books	girls

Try talking to your partner in your language.
Write a sentence or two in it.

Sign language

This is how you say the numbers in British Sign Language (BSL).

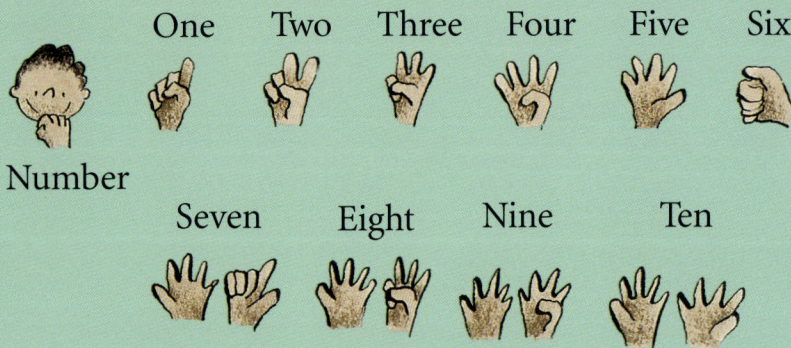

One   Two   Three   Four   Five   Six

Number

Seven   Eight   Nine   Ten

BSL is very widely used by deaf people, who can have difficulty understanding spoken English. For many deaf people BSL is their mother tongue.

You can find more BSL signs on **C** 13–14.

All about Poppy

Poppy was a hairy scary troll. She had razzle dazzle spectacles and great green eyes.

She liked to go out in the deep dark night.

Poppy wanted to go to the fair.

"The lights are too bright, Poppy dear," said her hairy scary mum. "Play by the deep dark river."

"No," said Poppy, glaring over her razzle dazzle spectacles. "I want to go to the fair."

"The music is too loud, Poppy dear," said her hairy scary dad. "Play in the deep dark wood."

"No," said Poppy, opening her deep dark eyes very wide. "I want to go to the fair."

Poppy was cross. She scowled from her razzle dazzle spectacles and made a very fierce face.

"Then I'll go by myself," she said.

And off she went.

From *The Day Poppy Went Out* by Moira Andrew, illustrated by Alison Forsythe (LBP Fiction 2, Band 2)

Talkabout

Adjectives

There are lots of **adjectives** in the extract about Poppy, and they are very important to the story. This is what the beginning looks like if the adjectives are covered up. (We have written all the nouns in bold print.)

> **Poppy** was a ⬛ **troll**. She had ⬛ **spectacles** and ⬛ **eyes**. She liked to go out in the ⬛ **night**.

Read the story without the adjectives. Does it make sense?
What are the missing adjectives and which nouns do they tell you about?
Why are they important to the story?

Here are some more nouns from the extract:

> lights   mum   river   music
> eyes   woods   face

Here are some more adjectives from the extract:

> hairy   scary   bright   fierce
> loud   wide   deep   dark

Which adjectives go with which nouns in the extract?

In the story some of the adjectives which tell you more about Poppy are:

> hairy   scary   cross   fierce

Think of some more good adjectives for Poppy.

Think of some adjectives to tell us about:

> you   Gregorie Peck   King Grumpyguts
> your classroom   a fairground

An adjective tells you more about a noun

1 Think of good adjectives to finish these sentences about you:

My hair is _____

My eyes are _____

I think I am quite _____

I am a very _____ person.

When I get up in the morning I feel _____.

At school I think I am very_____.

When I go to sleep at night I have _____ dreams.

2 Look back at *King Grumpyguts* on pages 12–13. Write down the adjectives which tell you more about these nouns. We have done the first one to show you how.

Page 12   a) king – grumpy   Page 13   a) park

b) palace   b) motorbike

c) gardens   c) king

3 Look back to Billy Blue (page 16)
Write down 3 adjectives to describe each of the nouns from the picture.
We have done the first one to show you how.
a) Billy Blue smiling, rosy-cheeked, young
b) the hippos
c) the crocodiles
d) Sam
e) the sea

4 Copy out this bit about Poppy on the ghost train and underline the adjectives. There are 5.

Poppy wheeled into the deep dark tunnel. "Whoo, whoo, whoo!" went a flappy snappy ghost. But Poppy was not frightened.

Into
Action

An adjective bank

- Make an adjective bank for your table. Find or make a box the right size for holding postcards.

- Get a postcard for each letter of the alphabet, label them and put them in alphabetical order.

- Collect as many adjectives as you can for each letter, and write them on the cards. They will come in handy when you are thinking up or writing stories.

There are lots of games you can play with your adjectives too, like Blind Man's Adjective. (One person closes his/her eyes, takes out a card, and points to it. The other person has to act out the adjective nearest to the pointer's finger.)

Whenever you come across another good adjective, add it to the bank.

Snow Palace

Beside a black and frozen lake
The palace of the Queen of Snow
Is guarded by the pointed peaks
Of icy mountains row on row.
And in the moonlight cold and keen
Like giants huge the mountains stand
Each with his spear of deadly steel
Gripped hard within his loyal hand.

James Reeves

Make a big picture of the Snow Palace, making sure you get the feel of all the adjectives in the poem.

Then make a picture of the Snow Queen. Write a list of good adjectives to describe your Queen.

The headteacher's cat

- Any number of people can play this game.
- Choose a letter of the alphabet.
- Each player has to think of an adjective to describe the cat, starting with the chosen letter (the sillier and funnier the better!)
- If you can't think of an adjective, you're out.
- If no one can think of an adjective, choose another letter.

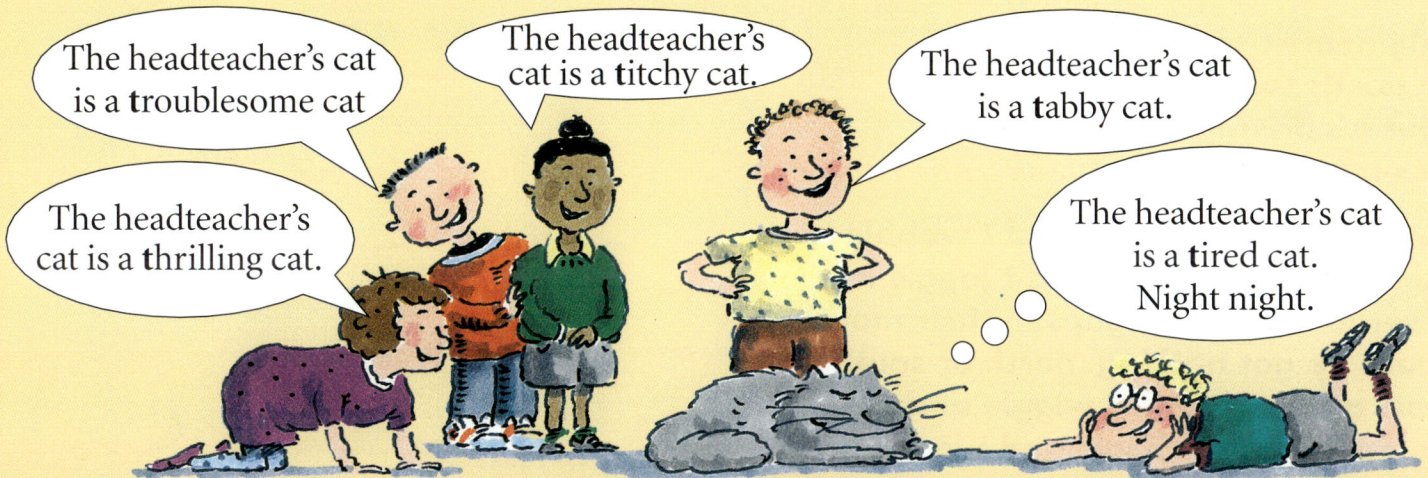

The headteacher's cat is a **t**roublesome cat

The headteacher's cat is a **t**itchy cat.

The headteacher's cat is a **t**abby cat.

The headteacher's cat is a **t**hrilling cat.

The headteacher's cat is a **t**ired cat. Night night.

Rhyming adjectives

The author of the Poppy stories likes rhyming words, especially adjectives:

reelly wheely chair   **flappy snappy** ghost   **hairy scary** troll

The person who wrote this little poem about the seasons liked rhyming adjectives as well:

**Spring is showery, flowery, bowery
Summer – hoppy, croppy, poppy
Autumn – wheezy, sneezy, freezy
Winter – nippy, drippy, slippy**

Anon

Write down as many adjectives as you can that rhyme with the ones below. You can make up new adjectives, as long as you know exactly what they mean:

dusty   foggy   silly   happy   blowy   rosy

Use some of your adjectives to write a little rhyming poem.

Jilly, now and then

From "Loose tooth"

I've got a loose tooth
and it's making me mad,
a loose tooth
and it's sure to go bad.

My dentist says that
it needs to come out
but it's driving me wild,
it's making me shout:

Loose tooth, I wiggle and I wobble it
Loose tooth, I jiggle and I joggle it,
Everyone else has gaps in their mouth
but I've got nothing, north or south
just a loose tooth, I wiggle and I wobble it,
a loose tooth, I jiggle and I joggle it...

I wobble it north
and I wobble it south
till that loose tooth
just wiggles
    and
wiggles
    wiggles
        wiggles
        wiggles
        wiggles
            wiggles
right out of my mouth!

From "Rocket Horse"

"I've got a rocket horse," said Jilly.
Her friends laughed, "Don't be silly."

"It's a rocking horse, like any other."
But Jilly just smiled and so did her brother...

Then off they zoomed far into space
past the moon with a smile on his face

On they flew to the planet Mars
with rocket horse jumping from star to star.

"I'm hungry" said Jilly, "It's time to go,"
So they rode very fast down a rainbow

all the way home.

From *Jilly's Days* by Brian Moses, illustrated by Bill Piggins (LBP Fiction 2, Band 3)

Glossary Check

tense

present tense

past tense

Talkabout

Present and past tenses

Which of Jilly's poems sounds as if it is happening now?
Which sounds as if it happened some time ago?

Find the verbs in the snippets below, and decide whether
they are in the **past tense** or the **present tense**:

My dentist says...   ...said Jilly   off they zoomed

it's making me mad   her friends laughed   it needs to come out

In *Rocket Horse*, most verbs are in the past tense, but some are in the present.
Which ones are they, and why do you think they are in the present tense?

Look back through all the extracts in this book and say whether they are written mainly in the past
tense or the present tense. Which tense makes writing sound more like a story?

All about Poppy on page 47 is mostly in the past tense.
Can anyone read it out, changing it into the present as they go?

The poem *My Shadow* on page 42 is mostly in the present tense .
Can anyone read it out, changing it into the past as they go?

Practice

When did it happen?
Verbs and tense

1 Copy these sentences with the verbs in the present tense, then write
the same sentences again, this time in the past tense. We have done
the first one to show you how.

Present	Past
I <u>run</u> home .	I <u>ran</u> home .
He <u>jumps</u> up .	
She <u>bangs</u> the door .	
He <u>helps</u> me .	
You <u>say</u> my name .	
I <u>swim</u> well .	
You <u>come</u> back .	

2 Copy these sentences with the verbs in the past tense, then write them in the present.

Past tense	Present tense
I went out.	I go out.
You made a cake.	
He looked up.	
I played out.	
She called me.	
He thought about it.	

More practice/revision: **C** 16
Link to *Spelling and Handwriting Workbook Two*, pages 18–20

Into Action

Me, past and present

Think of something that happened to you when you were much younger.

For instance,

- your first day at school,
- your 3rd or 4th birthday
- something funny that happened when you were a baby.

Draw a picture of yourself at that time.
Write about what happened.
Label the picture and the writing like this

Me in the past

Then draw a picture of yourself now.
Write about what you are like now

- your appearance
- your likes and dislikes
- the things you do in your spare time.

Label the picture and the writing like this

Me in the present

Hens

Gregorie Peck
plucked up
all her courage:
pluck-pluck-pluck.

She marched over to the big red egg.
" I shall sit on the egg until it
hatches or until the mother comes."
It was her finest hour.

So Gregorie pulled out
the shining red egg
from under the cart,
and climbed on to its
squeaky red dome.

It wasn't easy,
but she did it.

From *Gregorie Peck* by Geraldine McCaughrean, illustrated by Colin Smithson (LBP Fiction 1, Band 1)

and eggs

Hens are kept for laying eggs

People tamed hens thousands of years ago because they wanted eggs to eat.
They bred the hens to lay lots of eggs.

⬆ Most hens live in flocks without male birds.

The hens we keep now are different from wild birds. Tame hens lay eggs that do not have baby birds inside them. These hens can lay eggs nearly every day.

⬆ Jungle fowl were the first birds that people kept for their eggs.

From *Hens' eggs* by Jane Inglis (LBP Non-Fiction 1–Food)

Talkabout

The language of fiction and non-fiction

Which of the extracts on pages 56–57 is **fiction** and which is **non-fiction**? How do you know? What **facts** do you learn from the non-fiction extract?

Find as many differences as you can between the two extracts – differences which show you that one is **fiction** and the other is **non-fiction**.

Glossary Check

fiction

non-fiction

fact

Think about

- why the extract was written (What was the author trying to do?)

- the authors' choice of words
  (Any differences in the sort of nouns? adjectives? verbs? tense?)

- the illustrations (What was the artist trying to do?)

- the page layout (The position of the print? the pictures?)

- the title (Does it sound like a story or facts?)

Glossary Check

illustration

layout

title

Check that you know the meanings of the words in the magnifying glass below. Which of them go mainly with fiction and which go with non-fiction?

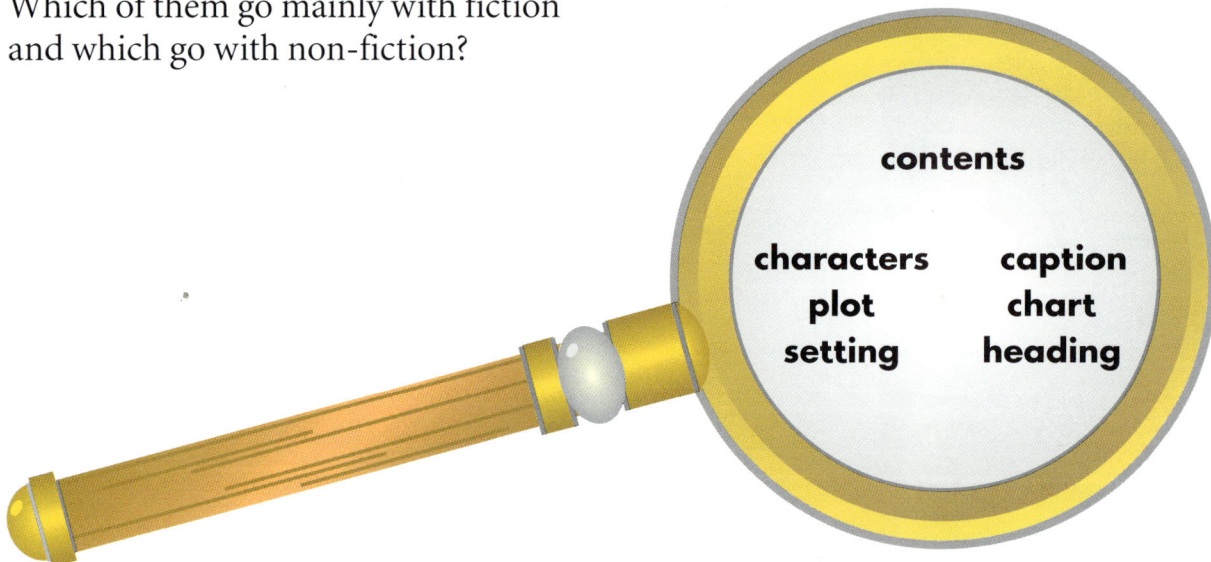

contents

characters   caption
plot   chart
setting   heading

Look back at all the other extracts in this book. What features tell you whether they are fiction or non-fiction? Find examples of all the words in the magnifying glass.

1 Find 3 non-fiction books in your class library.
Write 2 sentences about each book, like this

a) <u>Hens' eggs</u> is a non-fiction book by Jane Inglis.

b) It gives facts about hens, how to keep them, and what their eggs are like.

2 Find 3 fiction books in your class library.
Write 2 sentences about each book, like this

a) <u>Gregorie Peck</u> is a fiction book by Geraldine McGaughrean.

b) It is a story about a hen who wants to lay a big egg.

Link to *Spelling and Handwriting Workbook Two*, pages 21–22

Into Action

Animal fact and animal fiction

Choose an animal to write about.
Write two pages about it, one fiction page and one non-fiction page.

The fiction page will be a story.
The non-fiction page will be facts.
Set out the pages so that they look like fiction and non-fiction.

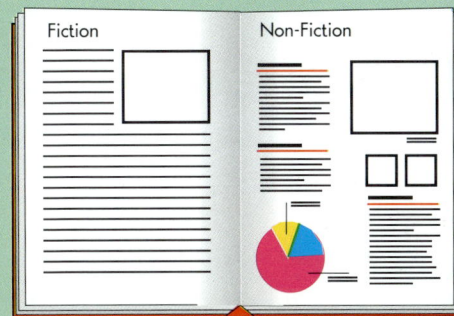

Use language which makes the pages sound like fiction and non-fiction.

If you are going well, you could write more than one page for each type of writing.

The egg

Let's think of eggs.
They have no legs.
Chickens come from eggs
But they have legs.
The plot thickens;
Eggs come from chickens,
But have no legs under 'em.
What a conundrum!

Ogden Nash

Is poetry fiction or non-fiction?
Write a poem about your animal to go with your fiction and non-fiction pages.
It does not have to rhyme.

Glossary of words about language
by David Crystal

adjective

An **adjective** is a word which goes with a noun and tells us something else about it.

Example: Poppy was a **hairy scary** troll. (See page 47)

bilingual

A **bilingual** person is someone who speaks two languages equally well.

Example: Letang speaks English and Setswana. (See page 44)

bold print

Bold print is darker and thicker than normal print. It is used to make words stand out on the page.

Example: **This sentence is in bold print.**

capital letter

The **capital letters** are:

A B C D E F G H I J K L M N O P Q R S T U V W X Y Z

caption

A **caption** is a piece of language written in small letters next to a picture or cartoon to explain what is happening in it.

Example: On page 20 the first caption is "This bread has just been sliced."

character

A **character** is a person in a story or a play. Sometimes other beings can be characters, such as animals or robots.

Example: Gregorie Peck is a character in a play. (See page 24)

chart

A **chart** is a special list, drawing or map which helps us to find something.

Example: On page 7 there is a chart showing "How a baby develops".

consonant

In writing, a **consonant** is any letter except A,E,I,O,U.

contents

The **contents** of a book is a list at the beginning which tells us what the main parts of the book are and the pages on which we can find them.

Example: The contents page in this book is on page 3.

dots

Three **dots** (...) show that a sentence is unfinished.

Example: "My husband is too... too... too..." (see page 26)

emphasis

Emphasis is the extra loudness we give to a word to show that it is specially important. When we **emphasize** a word, we say it more loudly than usual. In writing, we can write the word larger, write it in capital letters or underline it. In printed books, *italic print* is often used.

Example: "Now dance... *faster... FASTER!*" (see page 29)

exclamation   An **exclamation** is a kind of sentence which shows that we feel something very strongly.

Example: "You lazy, idle, good-for-nothing bird!" (see page 25)

exclamation mark   An **exclamation mark** is a special mark (!) at the end of a sentence which shows that the writer feels something very strongly.

Example: "Well! I don't know!" (see page 25)

expression   **Expression** is the way we show what we feel by using our face or voice. If we put some expression into our voice, we say things with more feeling.

extract   An **extract** is a piece of writing which has been taken from a longer work, such as a story or a play.

Examples: All the units in this book start with extracts. These extracts come from the fiction and non-fiction books in *The Longman Book Project*.

fact   A **fact** is something which really happened or which we know to be true. Our language is **factual** if we say it is based on facts.

fiction and non-fiction   **Fiction** is a kind of writing which tells you stories that have not really happened. The writer has made them up.
Non-fiction is a kind of writing which tells you about things that have really happened.

first language   A **first language** is the language we learned from our mother when we were babies. It is also called our **native language** or our **mother tongue.** Most people in Britain have English as a first language.

full stop   A **full stop** is a dot that shows the end of a sentence.

Example: The dot at the end of this sentence is a full stop.

glossary   A **glossary** is a list of special words and their meanings.

Example: *This* is a glossary of words about language.

heading   A **heading** is the words which stand out at the top of a piece of writing, or at the top of each part of it, which tell the reader what the writing is all about.

Examples: Every unit in this book has a heading.

On page 57 "Hens are kept for laying eggs"is a heading in an extract from a book.

illustration   An **illustration** is a picture or drawing which helps us explain something.

Examples: All the pictures in this book are illustrations.

instructions	When we give **instructions**, we tell people to do something, or teach them how to do something.
	Example: There are instructions on how to make an ABC book on page 15.
italic	If a piece of writing is printed in **italics,** all the letters are made to slope forwards. This makes the words stand out in a special way.
	Example: *This sentence is printed in italics.*
language	**Language** is what people use when they want to share their thoughts with each other. When they talk to each other, they use their voices to make words out of the sounds of speech. When they write to each other, they use their hands to make words out of letters.
layout	**Layout** is the way we set out a piece of writing on a page. It chiefly depends on the size we make our words and letters and the way we put space round them.
mother-tongue **native language** }	See **first language.**
non-fiction	See **fiction and non-fiction.**
noun	A **noun** is a word which gives a name to whatever we want to talk about. The names of people, places, things, animals and ideas are all nouns.
	Examples: king, country, car, lion,sadness
past tense	The **past tense** of a verb tells us what happened some time ago. Many verbs make their past tense by adding an -ed ending to the verb.
	Examples: laughed, zoomed, smiled, said, rode (see page 53)
plot	A **plot** is what happens in a story, such as in a book, a play, or a film.
	Example: The plot of the play *Cockadoodle-what?!* is– Cockerel Peck is too lazy to crow in the mornings, so the other animals try doing it for him. They fall over in the dark and their voices get muddled up. Gregorie Peck helps them sort out their voices, but ends up with the wrong voice herself.
present tense	The **present tense** of a verb tells us what is happening now.
	Examples: is making, says, wiggle, wobble (see page 52)
proper noun	A **proper noun** is a noun which is the name of one particular person, place, thing or idea. In writing, proper nouns begin with a capital letter.
	Examples: Jane, London, Ford Escort, Snoopy, Christmas.

punctuation	**Punctuation** is the set of marks which tell us how to read a piece of writing so that it makes sense. Punctuation also helps you read with expression. Examples of punctuation marks: **. ! ? , ...**
question	A **question** is a kind of sentence which people use when they want to know something. Example: Has it gone off? (and lots of other questions on page 20)
question mark	A **question mark** is a special mark (?) at the end of a sentence to show that someone has asked a question and wants to know something.
second language	A **second language** is a language we sometimes learn as well as our mother-tongue, so that we can talk to people in the place where we live.
sentence	A **sentence** is a piece of language which can stand by itself and make sense. In writing, the first word of a sentence begins with a capital letter. The last word is followed by a mark which shows the sentence has come to an end. It can be a full stop (.) a question mark (?) or an exclamation mark (!).
setting	The **setting** is the time and place in which something happens, such as the beginning of a story. Example: The setting of the play *Cockadoodle-What?!* is a farmyard very early in the morning.
statement	A **statement** is a kind of sentence which gives us information. Example: Here are some pictures of food. (Lots of other statements on page 20).
tense	A **tense** is the form of a verb which tells us if something is happening now, in the past, or in the future. **Present tense** and **past tense**.
title	A **title** is the name we give to a book, a painting, a play, or some other thing we have made. Example: After every extract, we give the title of the book it is taken from (see pages 6, 12, 16 and so on).
underlining	**Underlining** is a line we can draw under a piece of writing to show that it is important or special. Example: I'm too *tired.* *(page 26)*

verb	A **verb** is a word which tells us what is happening or what people are doing. Example: Dark shapes **are slipping** and **gliding** and **sliding** along. The shadows **dance.**
vowel	In writing, a **vowel** is one of the letters A, E, I, O, U and sometimes Y.
word	A **word** is any group of sounds or letters that can have a meaning. In writing, a word has a space on each side of it. In *very* slow speech, a word has silence on each side of it.